ANY NUMBER CAN PLAY

THE NUMBERS ATHLETES WEAR

George Sullivan

The Millbrook Press
Brookfield, Connecticut

12351557

Published by The Millbrook Press, Inc.
2 Old New Milford Road
Brookfield, Connecticut 06804
www.millbrookpress.com

Library of Congress Cataloging-in-Publication Data
Sullivan, George, 1933–
Any number can play: the numbers athletes wear / George Sullivan ;
illustrated by Anne Canevari Green.
p. cm.
Includes index.
Summary: Includes anecdotes recounting the history and lore
associated with the numbers on athletes' uniforms.
ISBN 0-7613-1557-8 (lib. bdg.)
1. Sports uniforms—History—Juvenile literature. 2. Sports uniforms—
Anecdotes—Juvenile literature. [1. Sports uniforms. 2. Sports—
History. 3. Sports—Miscellanea.] I. Green, Anne Canevari, ill. II. Title.
GV749.U53 S853 2000
796.'028—dc21 00-021476

introduction

As the 1998 baseball season entered its final stages, an electrifying home-run race developed between sluggers Mark McGwire of the St. Louis Cardinals and Sammy Sosa of the Chicago Cubs. Which one of the two would be the first to surpass Roger Maris's single-season mark of 61 home runs, one of the most revered of all sporting records?

Television cameras followed McGwire and Sosa everywhere. They were in the stadium parking lots before games and in the dressing rooms afterward. When either player emerged from the dugout to take a turn at the plate, the cameras zoomed in.

Reports of their home runs were carried on the front pages of newspapers across the country. Sports sections of newspapers featured special "Homer Watch" boxes.

On August 19, McGwire took over the lead from Sosa with a pair of home runs at Wrigley Field in Chicago. So began a home-run binge for McGwire that had him hitting 15 homers in 66 at bats.

McGwire smacked No. 59 just before the Cardinals began a five-game series against the Cubs at their home park, Busch Stadium. His 60th homer came on September 5. Only three players had ever hit as many as 60 home runs—Maris, of course, and Babe Ruth. Sosa at the time had 57.

McGwire hit No. 61 to tie Maris on September 7.

On the night of September 8, McGwire stepped into the batter's box with two out and no one on base in the fourth inning. Chicago's Steve Trachsel fired a sinking fastball. The 6-foot-5, 230-pound (196-cm, 104-kg) McGwire lashed out at the pitch, sending it low toward left field. The ball cleared the wall, caromed off an advertising sign, and dropped onto a walkway that circled the stadium beneath the seats.

McGwire's home-run production didn't stop at 62, nor did the home-run race. McGwire and Sosa continued to battle during the season's final weeks. McGwire, with a home-run blast on each of his final two at bats, boosted his total to 70, an undreamed-of figure. Sosa finished the season with 66.

With all those home runs, Mark McGwire lifted himself in the record book and earned himself a place in the baseball Hall of Fame. And, as *Sports Illustrated* noted, he also "made a permanent name for himself in American folklore."

The home-run duel had another effect. In the months that followed, baseball jerseys with McGwire's No. 25 and Sosa's No. 21

were sold by the hundreds of thousands to kids (and to grown-ups, too) who wanted to wear the number.

It happens all the time. When Michael Jordan, judged by many to be the greatest basketball player of all time, was helping to win championships for the Chicago Bulls, his No. 23 jersey was worn by kids everywhere basketball was played—and some places it wasn't played. Sports columnist Ira Berkow tells of friends of his on safari in Africa, who saw children come out of huts without electricity and running water wearing Jordan's No. 23 jersey.

It's the same with young female athletes. When the U.S. soccer team won the women's world title in 1999, sales of T-shirts and jerseys blazoned with Mia Hamm's No. 9 and Brandi Chastain's No. 6 surged.

To kids, the uniform number his or her favorite athlete wears is a serious matter. In May 1995, when Michael Jordan suddenly decided to change his uniform number to No. 23 from No. 45, a great ruckus resulted. All over Chicago, angry parents who had purchased No. 45 jerseys for their kids showed up at sporting goods stores demanding that the No. 45s be replaced with No. 23s. "I told them to hang on to their 45 jerseys," said one dealer. "They could be worth something someday."

As this suggests, uniform numbers are a direct link between a fan and his or her hero. There's something personal and satisfying about wearing a jersey that bears your favorite player's number.

The players themselves take uniform numbers even more seriously. Sometimes a player becomes attached to a certain number in high school or even earlier and may feel that the number has an effect on how he or she performs. It's something like wearing lucky socks or eating a certain food before a game.

When pitcher Roger Clemens signed with the Toronto Blue Jays in 1997, he presented Carlos Delgado with a Rolex watch worth

$15,900 in exchange for his No. 21. That was the number that Clemens had worn during his many seasons of success with the Boston Red Sox.

Ricky Henderson, traded to Toronto from the Oakland Athletics in 1993, paid out $25,000 to Blue Jays outfielder Turner Ward for the rights to No. 24.

Not every player has to go to such extremes to get the number he cherishes. First baseman Steve Garvey, in the fourteen years he spent with the Los Angeles Dodgers, always wore No. 6. When Garvey left the Dodgers to sign with the San Diego Padres in 1983, Tim Flannery was wearing No. 6. All Garvey had to do was buy Flannery a new suit to get him to give up his number.

This book takes a lighthearted look at uniform numbers. While it is meant to inform you, explaining how the use of numbers began and examining the strict numbering systems that some leagues follow, it is mostly meant to entertain. You'll get some fun along with the facts. Enjoy!

college codes

The NCAA (National Collegiate Athletic Association) "strongly recommends" that football jerseys be numbered from 1 through 99 according to this diagram:

80–99	70–79	60–69	50–59	60–69	70–79	80–99
O	O	O	O	O	O	O
End	Tackle	Guard	Center	Guard	Tackle	End

O
Quarterback

O   Backs   O
Halfback   1–49   Halfback

O
Fullback

Two other NCAA rules are meant to avoid number trickery. Players are not permitted to change numbers during a game. Nor are players on the same team permitted to wear the same number at the same time on the same down. Just imagine the confusion that could cause!

favored treatment

In ice hockey, it's traditional for the goalie to wear No. 1. In any given season, for example, more than half of all NHL (National Hockey League) teams follow the custom.

Three teams—the Chicago Blackhawks, Detroit Red Wings, and Philadelphia Flyers—have retired No. 1 to honor, respectively, Glenn Hall, Terry Sawchuk, and Bernie Parent, all goaltenders.

The reason goalies wear No. 1 goes back to an earlier period in the sport, to the 1930s and 1940s. In those days, teams traveled from one city to another by train. On overnight trips, players slept in railroad-car berths. These were narrow, built-in platform beds, one stacked above the other. Since one could sleep better in the bottommost berth, that's what every player tried to get.

But there weren't enough lower berths for every player who wanted one. Then someone came up with the idea of assigning berths according to uniform numbers. No. 1 would be given first choice in sleeping accommodations, No. 2 second choice, and so forth. This system assured that the senior members of the team, those who traditionally wore the lowest numbers, would get the coveted bottom bunks.

Playing goalie in those days was rough and rugged business, just as it is today. Goalies were usually more exhausted than any of their teammates after games. It was agreed that the team's goalie

was more deserving of a bottom bunk than any of the other players. So teams began assigning goalies the lowest number of all. Even though teams now travel by plane, the No. 1 tradition has lasted to this day.

a look back

The game of baseball, which has been traced all the way back to the 1840s, was played for almost a century before teams got around to putting numbers on players' backs. The New York Yankees, who began wearing numbers in 1929, was the first team to use them regularly.

Numbering players had been tried as early as 1888, however, when the Cincinnati Reds wore numbers on their sleeves. But the idea failed to catch on. The Cleveland Indians experimented with sleeve numbers in 1916, and the St. Louis Cardinals tried them in 1924. In each case, the numbers lasted for only the season.

When the Yankees put numbers on the backs of players in 1929, the club had each man's number correspond to his position in the batting order. Babe Ruth batted third, and Lou Gehrig was the cleanup hitter for the 1929 Yankees. That's how Ruth wound up with No. 3 and Gehrig with No. 4. These came to rank as two of the most famous numbers in baseball history.

Here's the complete lineup for the 1929 Yankees:

No. 1: Earl Combs, center field
No. 2: Mark Koenig, third base
No. 3: Babe Ruth, right field
No. 4: Lou Gehrig, first base

No. 5: Bob Meusel, left field
No. 6: Tony Lazzeri, second base
No. 7: Leo Durocher, shortstop
No. 8: Nig Grabowski, catcher

The second-string catcher was assigned No. 9. Pitchers were given Nos. 10 through 19, and nonregular players had to wear Nos. 20 and beyond.

Opening Day for the Yankees in 1929 was set for Tuesday, April 16, with the Boston Red Sox furnishing the opposition, but the game was canceled by rain. The teams were rained out the next day, too. Finally, on Thursday, April 18, the teams got a chance to play, although the day was cold and gray. The Yanks won, 7–3, with Ruth and Gehrig hitting homers.

No team in baseball was better than the Yankees during this time. They had captured three straight American League pennants and won the World Series in 1927 and 1928.

"When the Bronx Bombers sneezed in those days," *Sports Illustrated* once noted, "the rest of the league said, 'Bless you.'" Just about every other team followed the lead of the Yankees and began numbering its players by the next season.

two for the money

At the Indianapolis 500, the most famous auto race in the world, put your money on No. 2 or No. 3. In eighty-three runnings of the race (through 1999), No. 2 and No. 3 each won eight times, more than any other number. No. 1 was close, with seven wins. No. 14 had six victories, the most recent in 1999, when Kenny Brack won.

The numbers to avoid are 10, 11, 13, 18, 19, and anything in the 50s, except 51. They've never won.

moneymaker

In 1908, well before uniform numbers came into general use in college football, the University of Pittsburgh began numbering its backfield players—the quarterback, fullback, and two halfbacks. According to *The History of American Football*, the innovation was the work of Karl Davis, the team's publicity manager. Davis had been given the rights to print and sell programs for Pitt games.

Davis had a gimmick. He made sure the players wore different jerseys for each game. That meant that a new program had to be purchased each week in order for the fans to be able to identify the backfield players. Fortunately for the sports fans, who might prefer to spend their money on hot dogs, peanuts, or souvenirs, Davis's idea never caught on.

a helmetful of numbers

Jersey numbers in college football were first used around the turn of the century. But teams followed no standard policy. Some teams wore numbers; others didn't bother. And on still other teams, only the captain had a number. It appeared on the front of his jersey. It was usually 1 or 0.

According to Dr. L. H. Baker, writing in *Football Facts & Figures*, the first time that two teams with numbered jerseys lined up against one another was in 1913. The teams were the University of Wisconsin and the University of Chicago.

After that, the use of numbers spread fast. When the NFL (National Football League) set up shop in the early 1920s, virtually every team numbered its players. One reason was money. The numbers were printed in programs that were sold to fans. Teams struggled to survive in those days. Programs represented a source of much-needed income.

A pro player usually wore whatever jersey the team's equipment manager happened to toss him. If a player changed teams, he usually got a different number. And players' numbers usually differed from one season to the next, even if they stayed with the same team.

The great Jim Thorpe, for instance, who played as a running back for several teams in pro football's earliest days, is known to have worn at least three different numbers: 1, 3, and 21.

Steve Owen, who entered pro football in the 1930s as a lineman and coach for the New York Giants, is usually identified with No. 55. But Owen also wore 9, 36, and 44 during his career.

Football's number champion is Johnny "Blood" McNally, a halfback and one of football's original free spirits. McNally played for such teams as the Milwaukee Badgers, Duluth Eskimos, Pottsville Maroons, and Green Bay Packers. As he moved from one club to the next, he kept wearing different numbers, at least seven of them, including 10, 14, 15, 20, 24, 55, and 57. Four numbers more and McNally would have had enough for an entire team.

hexed

Ralph Branca, a pitcher for the Brooklyn Dodgers in the 1940s and early 1950s, is the player most closely linked to No. 13 and the bad luck it supposedly bestows. "I got No. 13 when I was a rookie in 1944," Branca once recalled. "The clubhouse man said it was the only uniform my size, but that if I was superstitious I could change it. I decided to keep it. I thought it might be lucky."

The number was no factor in Branca's early years with the team. In 1947 he won 21 games. "Not many pitchers ever do that," he once noted.

Branca's luck changed in 1951. By mid-August that year, the Dodgers were leading the second-place New York Giants by 13 1/2 games in the National League pennant race. Then the Giants began chipping away at the big Dodger lead. In one of the most stunning comebacks in baseball history, the Giants tied the Dodgers on the final day of the season. A three-game playoff resulted. The Giants won the first game, the Dodgers the second.

In the bottom of the ninth inning of the third and deciding game, with the Dodgers leading 4–2, Branca was called in from the bullpen to replace the starting pitcher. Bobby Thomson was the batter. Two men were on base. There was one out. Branca's first pitch was a strike. The pitcher then fired a fastball. Thomson lofted a high fly into left field that plopped into the stands for a home run. The Giants had won the pennant. Their joyous fans streamed out onto the field.

Branca turned and started for the clubhouse, his shoulders slumped. Never had misfortune struck a baseball player so swiftly and so surely. Branca, wearing No. 13, had tempted fate and lost.

When Branca reported to training camp in the spring of 1952, a No. 12 jersey was waiting for him. The club had put his No. 13 into storage.

with due respect

Humble, as defined in dictionaries, means being modest, not proud. Bill Walton, 6 feet 11 (211 cm), from La Mesa, California, an exceptional center in both college and professional basketball, was humble in picking out his uniform numbers.

At UCLA in the early 1970s, Walton wore No. 32. The reason: Lew Alcindor, a three-time All America selection with the Bruins, had worn No. 33. Walton explained that he did not feel he was quite the equal of Mr. Alcindor (who, as Kareem Abdul-Jabbar, went on to become a superstar with the Los Angeles Lakers), and thus his number should be one digit less than Alcindor's.

Wearing No. 32, Walton led UCLA to the NCAA title in 1972 and 1973. Following college, Walton embarked on a pro career with the Portland Trail Blazers, where he continued to wear No. 32.

The Boston Celtics acquired Walton in 1985. Again he wanted to wear No. 32, but Kevin McHale owned it. In picking out a new number, Walton used the same reasoning he had used during his college years. He realized that in joining the Celtics as their center he was following in the footsteps of the great Bill Russell, who wore No. 6. Walton's choice was—you guessed it—No. 5.

number Chaos

During his 12 1/2 years with the Chicago Bulls, Michael Jordan captured nine individual scoring titles, won five Most Valuable Player awards, averaged 31.7 points per game, the highest career average in NBA history, and led his team to 6 titles in his last eight seasons. He is generally considered to be the greatest player in basketball history.

Jordan was well known for shaving his head clean, favoring red sneakers, and wearing No. 23. He once explained how he happened to adopt that number. "My favorite number had always been No. 45, which was my older brother Larry's number. But when I got to high school, I couldn't have No. 45 because Larry had it. So I decided to have half of his number—22 1/2, which rounded off is 23. That's how I came to wear No. 23."

Jordan was still wearing No. 23 when, following the 1993 season, he left basketball to attempt a career in baseball, a decision that sent shock waves through the world of sports. Jordan was assigned to the minor league Birmingham Barons. Before long, it became apparent that he did not have the kind of talent necessary to succeed as a .300 hitter in the major leagues. Once he had accepted that fact, he decided to return to the Bulls.

Jordan had worn No. 45, his original favorite, during the summer he spent with the Birmingham Barons. When he went back to the Bulls in mid-March 1995, he shunned his old No. 23 in favor of No. 45.

Jordan's comeback was not immediately successful. There were times he flashed his old magic, but mostly he looked rusty and in the late stages of games sometimes appeared winded.

One of Jordan's most dismal performances came in the first game of the Eastern Conference semifinals, which the Bulls lost to the Orlando Magic. After the game, Jordan announced that he was switching back to jersey No. 23. He said that he would feel more comfortable with that number. "No. 23 is me," he said, "so why try to be something else?"

But Jordan's decision angered officials of the National Basketball Association. "We can't have a situation where a player can decide every night what number he wants to wear," said a league spokesperson. "It would be mass chaos if everyone did that."

The league announced that the Bulls were being fined $25,000 for allowing Jordan to change his number in midseason. And the team would continue to be fined at the rate of $25,000 per game if Jordan did not switch back to No. 45.

Jordan had no thought of backing down. "He really wants to wear No. 23 right now," said Phil Jackson, the Chicago coach.

The Bulls supported Jackson, defying the league. Said Jerry Reinsdorf, the owner of the team: "It is extremely important to Michael that he be permitted to wear his original number, and after discussions with all involved, the Bulls have concluded that we will issue No. 23 to Michael for the balance of the playoffs."

With the backing of his team, Jordan went on wearing No. 23. However, when Orlando quickly eliminated the Bulls from the playoffs, the controversy died. Jordan did not shine in the playoffs, often failing in crucial moments. Afterward, he said he was "disappointed."

Once the season ended, the NBA fined the Bulls an additional $100,000 for permitting Jordan to change his jersey number. The team had earlier been fined $25,000. The added $100,000 penalty broke down to $25,000 a game for the four additional games in which Jordan continued to wear No. 23.

That amounted to a total of $125,000 in fines. In all of sports history, never had wearing a certain uniform number come at such a high price. And unless another Michael Jordan comes along, it's not likely to happen again.

breaking barriers

Just about every major-league baseball team has its collection of retired numbers to honor all-time great players. There's one player who has had his number retired by every team in both the American and National Leagues. What is the number? Who is the player?

Answer: It's number 42, worn by Jackie Robinson, who broke baseball's color barrier as a member of the Brooklyn Dodgers. Major-league baseball retired the number in 1997.

honored, honored, and honored

Nolan Ryan, whose explosive fastball was clocked at better than 100 miles (160 km) per hour, is the all-time major-league leader in strikeouts, with 5,714 of them. Steve Carlton, second on the all-time list with 4,136, is more than 1,500 strikeouts behind.

For this and his many other notable feats, three major-league teams retired the numbers that Ryan wore. The California Angels retired his No. 30, the Texas Rangers also retired his No. 30, and the Houston Astros, the No. 34 he wore with that team.

Ryan spent his early years in the majors with the New York Mets, but the team has yet to announce that it is taking out of service the No. 30 he wore as a member of the team. Still, having your uniform number retired by three teams is quite an honor. By the year 2000, no other player had achieved it.

jinxed or not?

Fear of the number thirteen—what is known as triskaideka-phobia—is quite common. The floor-button panels in the elevators of many tall buildings often don't show a number 13. They read: " … 10, 11, 12, 14, 15, 16. … "

Commercial airlines refuse to have a Flight 13. Aboard their planes, no seats or rows of seats are assigned that number.

When it comes to uniform numbers in professional sports, it's much the same. No. 13 is usually avoided. This is especially true in the National Hockey League. In most seasons, No. 13 is a rarity. And the few players who do happen to wear the number are almost always European-born.

All those hockey players who avoid No. 13 may have in mind what happened to Lars Lindgren, who played defense for the Vancouver Canucks. Lindgren got hurt so often that he believed he was the victim of an injury jinx. In an effort to change his luck, Lindgren changed from jersey No. 3 to 13. He stopped getting injured, but during a game in November 1982 against the Edmonton Oilers, Lindgren shot the puck into his own net.

Baseball players are more willing to challenge the hex. In any given season, about half of all major-league teams have a player who wears No. 13.

Second baseman Edgardo Alfonzo of the New York Mets wore No. 13. In 1999 he had an outstanding season, playing flawless defense and hitting the ball consistently and with power. Curiously, Alfonzo had a 12-inch (30-cm) Bart Simpson doll hanging in his locker. Maybe that doll counteracted the No. 13 hex.

In professional football, 13 is ordinarily a quarterback's number. But it is seldom seen.

In avoiding the number, quarterbacks may have Dan Marino in mind. In almost two decades as quarterback for the Miami Dolphins, Marino always wore No. 13. At first glance, it didn't seem to have any effect upon his career. With his strong and accurate right arm, Marino came to own virtually every important NFL passing record. But one thing that he never got to own was a Super Bowl ring. There must have been times during his long career that Marino wondered whether the No. 13 on his back had anything to do with his failure to capture a championship.

The lack of successful players wearing No. 13 is made obvious by checking the retired uniform numbers. In baseball, basketball, football, and hockey, only two No. 13s have been retired.

The first No. 13 to be put on the shelf belonged to Don Maynard, a pass receiver for the New York Jets during the 1960s and into the 1970s. Maynard was skilled at taking the passes he caught and turning them into long gains. During his career, he averaged 18.7 yards per catch. If pass receivers were ranked on the basis of average yards gained per reception (instead of number of receptions), Don Maynard would be No. 1.

Basketball's Wilt Chamberlain was another player who success-fully defied the No. 13 jinx. Chamberlain, who played for the Philadelphia 76ers and several other NBA teams, retired in 1972.

Chamberlain practically rewrote the record book. He scored 31,419 points during his career, second only to Kareem Abdul-Jabbar's 38,387 points, but 2,142 more than Michael Jordan with 29,277 points. And Chamberlain grabbed 23,924 rebounds, still the record. In one game, Chamberlain actually scored 100 points. During the 1962 season, Chamberlain averaged 50.4 points per game, a mark no other player has approached. For Wilt Chamberlain, No. 13 was anything but unlucky.

banned

26 48 58 62 87 94. In what major American sport are players prohibited from wearing these numbers?

It's basketball. In both college and professional basketball, uni-form numbers rarely include any double-digit number that is higher than 55. Numbers 6, 7, 8, and 9, as part of double-digit num-bers are as rare as 5-foot (152-cm) All Stars.

It's not hard to understand why this is so. It has to do with the way in which the referee communicates with the official scorer during a game. When a foul occurs, the referee halts play, turns toward the scorer's table, and indicates the uniform number of the player who has committed the foul with a hand signal. For example, if the player's number is 24, the referee holds up two fingers on his or her left hand and four fingers on the right hand. That means "two four"—or 24—to the scorer.

But suppose the player who did the fouling was wearing No. 27. The 7 would cause a problem. How would the referee signal a 7 with a hand that has only four fingers and a thumb?

In professional basketball, there is no official rule saying that double-digit uniform numbers cannot include digits greater than 5. "It's a tradition we follow," says a spokesperson for the National Basketball Association. "Theoretically, a player could wear any number."

Despite the absence of an official rule, few teams ever issue double-digit numbers that include 6, 7, 8, or 9. The most notable exception was the Minneapolis Lakers in the case of George Mikan, a dominant figure in pro basketball's early years. Mikan, who retired in 1956, wore No. 99. When Mikan fouled, the referee must have shouted out his number.

luck of the draw

On October 18, 1924, Harold "Red" Grange of the University of Illinois scored five touchdowns against a top-rated Michigan team. Grange wore No. 77 that day. For what he did that afternoon and for all that he accomplished as a running back in the years that followed, the number became forever identified with Grange. He was even sometimes referred to as "ol' 77."

John Underwood of *Sports Illustrated* once asked Grange how he happened to get his famous number. Grange recalled the first practice he attended as an Illinois freshman. "The guy in front of me got No. 76," Grange said. "The guy in back of me got 78."

the first

A big, quiet, and very determined man, Lou Gehrig began playing first base regularly for the New York Yankees on June 1, 1925. His batting feats have seldom been equaled. He hit 40 or more home runs five times. He twice led the American League with 49 homers. (The 184 runs he batted in during 1931 is still a league record.) He led the league in batting in 1934 with a .363 average and had a lifetime average of .340.

Year in, year out, Gehrig was at first base for the Yankees despite the assorted aches and pains ballplayers are subject to. He did not take himself out of the lineup until May 2, 1939. He had become too ill to play, because of a crippling disease that was to claim his life two years later. Between 1925 and 1939, Gehrig played in 2,130 consecutive games, an iron-man streak that remained a record until 1995, when surpassed by Baltimore's Cal Ripken.

On July 4, 1939, the Yankees held "Lou Gehrig Day" at Yankee Stadium, and his No. 4 uniform was retired. Gehrig, in his speech of appreciation, said he was "the luckiest man on the face of the earth."

The ceremony at Yankee Stadium marked the first time a club had ever taken a number out of use to honor a player. Other baseball teams and then teams in other sports soon began to adopt the practice.

in tribute

Among pro football running backs, No. 32 is held in the highest esteem. The number first became famous when worn by Hall of Famer Jim Brown, who set more than a dozen National Football League rushing records as a member of the Cleveland Browns

during the late 1950s and early 1960s. Many say that Brown is the best running back of all time.

A good number of Brown's records were eventually wiped out by O. J. Simpson, who had an exceptional career with the Buffalo Bills. Simpson, also a member of Pro Football's Hall of Fame, wore No. 32 in recognition of Brown and his many achievements.

Other running backs who have worn No. 32 include Franco Harris of the Pittsburgh Steelers, an outstanding performer for more than a decade beginning in 1972, and Ottis Anderson of the St. Louis Cardinals, the NFL's Rookie of the Year in 1979 and a fearsome runner in the years that followed.

Marcus Allen of the Los Angeles Raiders and, later, the Kansas City Chiefs, piled more glory on No. 32. Allen was voted the Most Valuable Player in Super Bowl XVIII in 1984 and was the NFL's leading rusher in 1985. Allen wore No. 32, not in remembrance of Jim Brown, but to honor O. J. Simpson, Allen's idol. Incidentally, both Allen and Franco Harris are Hall of Fame members.

As professional football entered the 21st century, Jamal Anderson of the Atlanta Falcons and Ricky Watters of the Seattle Seahawks carried on the No. 32 tradition. Both were consistently among pro football's leading ground-gainers as well as Hall of Fame candidates.

four-wheeled numbers

Stock-car racing has its numbers, too—the big, bold numbers that are painted on the sides of each car. To stock-car racing fans, some of these numbers are just as well known as Babe Ruth's No. 3 or Hank Aaron's No. 44.

Here are some of the best known:

No. 2 — Rusty Wallace, Rookie of the Year in 1984 and Winston Cup champion in 1989.

No. 3 — Dale Earnhardt, a longtime favorite of the fans and seven-time Winston Cup champion, which tied him with Richard Petty for the most career titles.

No. 5 — Terry Labonte, who, in 1996, broke Richard Petty's record of 514 consecutive starts.

No. 6 — Mark Martin, who had 22 wins in his first eleven seasons of driving, including a record four-in-a-row victories in 1993.

No. 17 — Darrell Waltrip, a three-time Winston Cup champion and the winner of more than $15 million in prize money.

No. 24 — Jeff Gordon, who rocketed to superstar status after winning honors as Rookie of the Year in 1993; holds three Winston Cup titles.

No. 43 — Richard Petty, onetime king of the stock-car drivers; his son Kyle drives car No. 42.

No. 88 — Dale Jarrett, who scored his first stock-car victory at Brooklyn, Michigan, in 1991; since then has ranked as one of racing's most solid performers.

No. 94 — Bill Elliott, who has 40 career victories and more than $16 million in earnings.

No. 98 — John Andretti, a member of one of stock-car racing's most famous families; began racing in go-carts at age 9.

following a formula

When Danny Buggs, a college football player at West Virginia University, arrived at the training camp of the New York Giants in the summer of 1975, he asked for jersey No. 8. "You can't wear No. 8," he was told. "You're a wide receiver. You have to wear a number in the 80s."

Buggs was given No. 86, which didn't make him happy. "No. 8 means a lot to me," he said. "I wore it in college. Our other wide receiver wore No. 9. It's psychological or something. I don't know. I feel lighter in 8; I feel faster."

Danny Buggs was no exception. Hundreds of pro football players are made to wear jersey numbers that have no particular meaning for them. That's because of the NFL's number-by-position policy. It states that players' jerseys must be numbered as follows:

Quarterbacks and kickers: 1 through 19
Running backs and defensive backs: 20 through 49
Centers and linebackers: 50 through 59
All linemen: 60 through 79
Wide receivers and tight ends: 80 through 89

Numbering by position, which the NFL introduced in 1972, was once tried by baseball's National League. Managers, coaches, and catchers were to wear numbers from 1 to 9; infielders, 10 to 19; outfielders, 20 to 29, and so forth. The players protested, however, preferring to keep the numbers that they had. Baseball abandoned the plan. Maybe Danny Buggs should have been a baseball player.

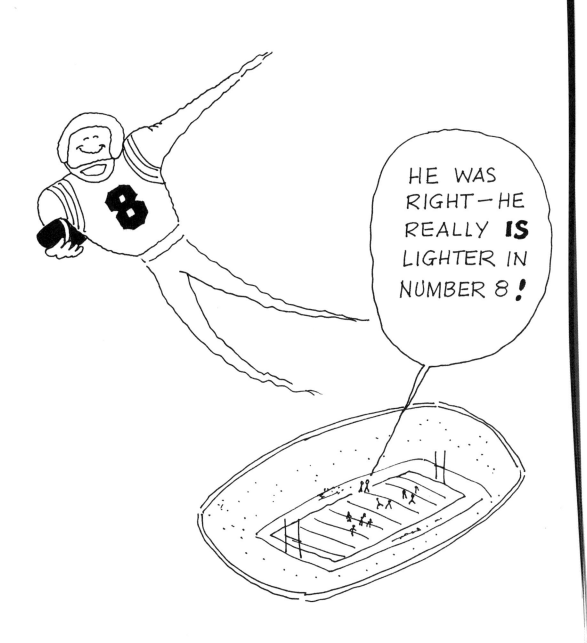

honored numbers

Since July 4, 1939, when the New York Yankees retired Lou Gehrig's No. 4 in the first ceremony of its type, some 123 baseball players, coaches, and managers have seen their numbers taken out of use.

No. 4 is the number that major-league teams have honored the most often. Eight players have seen their No. 4s pass into retirement. They are:

Luke Appling, Chicago White Sox
Joe Cronin, Boston Red Sox
Lou Gehrig, New York Yankees
Ralph Kiner, Pittsburgh Pirates
Paul Molitor, Milwaukee Brewers
Mel Ott, New York Giants
Duke Snider, Los Angeles Dodgers
Earl Weaver, Baltimore Orioles

Every number from 1 through 21 has been honored at least once, except Nos. 12 and 13.

The New York Yankees have retired fourteen numbers (honoring fifteen individuals), more than any other team. They are:

No. 1, Billy Martin
No. 3, Babe Ruth
No. 4, Lou Gehrig
No. 5, Joe DiMaggio
No. 7, Mickey Mantle
No. 8, Yogi Berra, Bill Dickey

No. 9, Roger Maris

No. 10, Phil Rizzuto

No. 15, Thurman Munson

No. 16, Whitey Ford

No. 23, Don Mattingly

No. 32, Elston Howard

No. 37, Casey Stengel

No. 44, Reggie Jackson

Three teams have yet to retire any numbers. They are the Tampa Bay Devil Rays, the Arizona Diamondbacks, and Toronto Blue Jays.

a city's number

To sports fans in Los Angeles, No. 32 is special. For one thing, it was the number worn by Sandy Koufax, baseball's best pitcher of the 1960s, a Hall of Famer, whose record includes four strikeout titles and four no-hitters, one of them a perfect game. Koufax was the National League's Most Valuable Player in 1963, one of the years he helped carry the Dodgers to victory in the World Series. He was also a major factor in 1965, when the Dodgers again captured the World Series and again in 1966, when the team won the National League pennant.

Basketball star Earvin "Magic" Johnson of the Los Angeles Lakers during the 1980s was another No. 32. A dazzling ball handler, Johnson was a vital cog in the Lakers' success beginning with his rookie season of 1979–1980. The team won the NBA title that season and again in 1981–1982, 1984–1985, 1986–1987, and 1987–1988.

Los Angeles had still another outstanding No. 32 in running back Marcus Allen of the Raiders. At the University of Southern California (in Los Angeles), Allen won the Heisman Trophy as the nation's best college player in 1981.

Allen was just as spectacular as a pro player. He rushed for a Super Bowl record of 191 yards in 1984, as the Los Angeles Raiders crushed the Washington Redskins, 38–9. The following season Allen led the NFL in ground-gaining, with 1,759 yards.

Looking back on all of this, one fan concluded: "You can't have a championship in Los Angeles without a great No. 32."

a new leaf

In baseball the higher a player's number, the lower his sense of security. Someone who wears, say, a 49, 56, or 62 on his back is usually a player on the brink, in danger of being sent to a minor-league team.

High numbers are distributed in the spring, when scores of young hopefuls join the veteran players at each team's training camp. Since the veterans have the numbers beginning with 1 and

continuing in sequence, the newcomers have to be satisfied with what remains. And what remains are numbers in the 50s, 60s, and 70s. Occasionally even an 80 or 90 is seen.

How, then, does one explain the No. 72 worn by catcher Carlton Fisk? After a decade as a star performer for the Boston Red Sox, Fisk became a free agent and signed with the Chicago White Sox in 1981. Fisk deserved a low number, perhaps an 8, a number often worn by catchers.

Fisk, however, felt that his switch from the Red Sox to the White Sox represented a real turnabout in his career. The change called for a new uniform number. In Boston, Fisk had always worn No. 27. So he turned it around, and the result was a number higher than that worn by any other major leaguer.

a name to remember

In 1986, when the San Francisco Giants were honoring the team's all-time greats, the club management ran into a problem. It had to do with pitcher Christy Mathewson, who had won 372 games as a member of the New York Giants and one game for the Cincinnati Reds—373 games overall. Mathewson also won 11 games in World Series play. Mathewson retired in 1916 and was named to baseball's Hall of Fame twenty years later.

The usual way the Giants paid tribute to their outstanding players was to paint their numbers on the right-field wall at Candlestick Park. These players had been so honored:

Bill Terry, No. 3
Mel Ott, No. 4
Carl Hubbell, No. 11

Willie Mays, No. 24
Juan Marichal, No. 27
Willie McCovey, No. 44

The problem with Mathewson was that he had no number to retire. He played in a time before uniforms carried numbers.

The Giants solved the problem by retiring Mathewson's name. Before an Old-Timers' game at Candlestick Park in 1986, a plaque with Mathewson's name on it went up on the wall.

"It's kind of unusual, retiring a name," said Pat Gallagher, a club vice president. "We talked for years about how to honor Mathewson. We felt this was the best way."

Someone then asked Gallagher what he would do if a young player ever showed up at spring training calling himself Christy Mathewson. Gallagher grinned. "We'd just have to come up with a new name for him," he said.

leading the way

Women players were still a rarity in most professional sports when, in 1986, 27-year-old Nancy Lieberman signed a contract with the Springfield (Massachusetts) Fame of the United States Basketball League. A 5-foot-10 (178-cm) point guard, Lieberman had first become nationally known as a three-time All-America selection at Old Dominion College in Norfolk, Virginia. In 1998, as Nancy Lieberman-Cline, she became the coach of the Detroit Shock of the WNBA (Women's National Basketball Association).

Growing up in Brooklyn, where she was born, Lieberman played playground basketball on asphalt courts. Her idol was slick Walt Frazier, the New York Knicks superstar who later was elected to basketball's Hall of Fame. As the first woman to play professional basketball, Lieberman chose to wear Frazier's number—No. 10.

number Shortage

When Jerry Sichting was traded from the Indiana Pacers to the Boston Celtics at the beginning of the 1985–1986 basketball season, he asked for No. 14. But the number had been retired, he was told. It was hanging from the rafters at the Boston Garden in honor of its last wearer, Bob Cousy, who had retired in 1963. Cousy has been cited often as the best playmaker in basketball history.

Since No. 14 wasn't available, Sichting asked for No. 24. That was gone, too. No. 24 had been retired to honor Sam Jones, a sharp-shooting guard during Boston's glory years of the 1960s. Sichting eventually settled for No. 12.

As this suggests, the Boston Celtics have paid tribute to a good many players over the years. They have, in fact, retired more num-

bers than any other basketball team, twenty of them. This isn't unusual when you consider that the Celtics, through 1999, had captured the National Basketball Association championship sixteen times. In other words, a great many Boston players have deserved to be honored.

Besides players, the Celtics have paid tribute to Walter Brown, the founder of the team. The No. 1 jersey was retired to honor Brown. No. 2 was put in retirement to honor Arnold "Red" Auerbach, the team's former coach, later its general manager and, still later, its president.

These are the twenty numbers retired by the Celtics:

No. 00, Robert Parish

No 1, Walter Brown

No. 2, Arnold "Red" Auerbach

No. 3, Dennis Johnson

No. 6, Bill Russell

No. 10, Jo Jo White

No. 14, Bob Cousy

No. 15, Tom Heinsohn

No. 16, Tom "Satch" Sanders

No. 17, John Havlicek

No. 18, Dave Cowens, Jim Loscutoff

No. 19, Don Nelson

No. 21, Bill Sharman

No. 22, Ed Macauley

No. 23, Frank Ramsey

No. 24, Sam Jones

No. 25, K. C. Jones

No. 32, Kevin McHale

No. 33, Larry Bird

No. 35, Reggie Lewis

At the rate they're going, the Boston Celtics may one day run out of numbers. The players might have to start wearing letters on their backs instead.

super number

Which team will win the next Super Bowl? If the past is any guide to the future, it could be the team whose quarterback wears No. 12.

Through the years, No. 12 wearers have accounted for nine Super Bowl triumphs. Winning quarterbacks who have worn No. 12 include Terry Bradshaw of the Pittsburgh Steelers, Bob Griese of the Miami Dolphins, Ken Stabler of the Oakland Raiders, and Joe Namath of the New York Jets.

Quarterback Jack Thompson of the Cincinnati Bengals was another No. 12 involved in a Super Bowl. He was a member of the Bengal squad that faced the San Francisco 49ers in Super Bowl XVI. But Thompson never got into the game. Maybe that's why the Bengals lost.

one of a kind

Jim Otto, a center for the Oakland Raiders, was a man of many accomplishments. He started every game played by the Oakland team during the ten-year history of the AFL (American Football League). He was the AFL's one and only All-League center. He was voted into Pro Football's Hall of Fame in 1980, the first year that he was eligible for enshrinement.

Despite his many achievements, Otto is probably remembered more for the No. 00 he wore than for anything else. (Otto was No. 50 during his rookie season. But always after, he was No. 00.)

"The guys on the team used to call me 'Ott,'" Otto once recalled. "That sounded like 'aught,' the word that means a cipher or zero. So the club decided that they would put a zero, a single zero, on my uniform."

At the time, however, a running back named Johnny Olszewski, who was nicknamed "Johnny O," was playing for the Washington Redskins of the NFL, and Olszewski was wearing an O. The Raiders didn't want Otto's number to be confused with Olszewski's letter, so they decided to give him two zeroes instead of one.

It was rare to see a uniform with No. 00 on it in those days, and Otto quickly became well known. But although the number earned him a certain distinction, he was often razzed by the fans because of it. "Otto, you're not nothing," one fan yelled, "you're *double nothing!*"

Another fan wanted to know whether the No. 00 represented Otto's I.Q.

Some of Otto's critics claimed the only reason he won All-League honors so many times was that he was so noticeable.

Otto shrugged off these criticisms. All the attention he got made up for it.

Otto retired from football in 1975. Originally from Wisconsin, he settled in Yuba City, California, where he became a successful businessman. He owned a restaurant and operated a land development company. And he drove a car with a license plate that read: I AM 00.

change of heart

During the years that the Colts played in Baltimore, they were one of the winningest teams in pro football. They captured several conference and division titles, the National Football League championship twice, and appeared in two Super Bowls, winning Super Bowl V.

Between the years 1953 and 1976, the Colts never failed to produce at least one All-Pro player, and in one year, 1959, they boasted eight of them.

Seven Baltimore Colts are members of Pro Football's Hall of Fame. And the club retired the jersey number of each. They were:

No. 19, Johnny Unitas
No. 22, Buddy Young
No. 24, Lenny Moore
No. 70, Art Donovan
No. 77, Jim Parker
No. 82, Raymond Berry
No. 89, Gino Marchetti

The Colts abandoned Baltimore after the 1983 season and moved to Indianapolis. There the team's earlier success caused a problem. The Baltimore equipment manager began to run out of jersey numbers. It wasn't just because so many numbers had been retired and thus had been taken out of use. Another factor was that rosters were much bigger in the 1980s than they had been in the 1960s. The equipment manager also had to contend with the league rule that required certain numbers for each position.

To help ease the number shortage, the Indianapolis Colts announced they planned to "unretire" the No. 82 once worn by Raymond Berry and the No. 89 worn by Gino Marchetti.

That was a mistake. Fans of the Colts and former Colt players protested. "This is about as low as you can get," said Jim Parker, a former lineman with the team (and whose No. 77 had been retired). "It's like digging up a grave."

Officials of the Indianapolis Colts changed their minds. They announced that No. 82 and No. 89 would stay retired.

Baltimore fans and former players seemed satisfied and calmed down. But they're on their guard. If Indianapolis ever lays a hand on those retired numbers again, you'll hear their screams.

hockey's highest

Since there are relatively few players on a hockey team's roster, there's no need for high jersey numbers. Indeed, numbers beyond the 40s are a rarity.

When you do see a high number, there's usually a good reason for it. For example, when Peter Klima, a forward for the Detroit Red Wings, picked out No. 85, he did it to commemorate 1985, the year he left his native Czechoslovakia to take up residence in the United States.

Mario Lemieux, a forward for the Pittsburgh Penguins, was greatly impressed by the awesome achievements of the great Wayne Gretzky, No. 99 for the Los Angeles Kings. Lemieux selected No. 66, Gretzky's number upside down. (The tale of Gretzky and his No. 99 is told later in this book.)

Two of the most noted high numbers were worn by a pair of New York Rangers: Phil Esposito, No. 77, and Ken Hodge, No. 88. The Rangers obtained both players from the Boston Bruins. Esposito had worn No. 7 in Boston, while Hodge had No. 8. Since other players were wearing their numbers when they arrived in New York, Esposito and Hodge settled on a double digit in order to be able to wear the single digit they wanted.

badge of honor

Sammy Sosa, the Chicago Cubs' awesome home-run hitter, wore No. 21. Why did Sosa wear that number?

Sosa wore No. 21 in honor of Roberto Clemente, a superstar outfielder for the Pittsburgh Pirates. Clemente won four batting

titles in his eighteen National League seasons and had a lifetime batting average of .317. He died tragically. Clemente took off from his native Puerto Rico on New Year's Eve, 1972, in a plane loaded with food and supplies for the victims of an earthquake in Managua, Nicaragua. The plane crashed into the sea. Clemente's body was never found. Within three months of his death, Clemente was elected to baseball's Hall of Fame.

sluggers' numbers

Hank Aaron, with 755 home runs, the all-time leader in that department, wore No. 44 throughout almost his entire career, which covered 23 seasons. By the time he retired in 1976, Aaron and No. 44 were closely linked in the public's mind.

Willie McCovey, tied with Ted Williams at tenth on the all-time homer list, with 521 homers, also wore No. 44. McCovey, who played for the San Francisco Giants, was voted in to baseball's Hall of Fame in 1986.

Reggie Jackson, another famous slugger, was yet another 44. Jackson, with 563 homers, is sixth on the all-time list.

Jackson didn't always wear No. 44. In the early years of his career, Reggie played for the Oakland A's and wore No. 9. He continued to wear that number until he was traded to the New York Yankees in 1976. There he found that No. 9 was being worn by third baseman Graig Nettles. It was then that Jackson chose No. 44, explaining that he would be wearing it out of respect for Aaron and McCovey and their achievements. "I'm in very good company," said Jackson.

basketball's best

In the years that he played for the NBA's Milwaukee Bucks and the Los Angeles Lakers, Kareem Abdul-Jabbar was a scoring machine, pouring in 35,387 points—more than any other player in the history of the game. He was a major force in the team's many championship seasons during the 1980s. Abdul-Jabbar retired in 1989.

Through his long career, Abdul-Jabbar wore No. 33. It was the most celebrated number in basketball until Michael Jordan's No. 23 became widely known.

On January 20, 1986, not long before the Lakers were to play the Chicago Bulls in Chicago, someone stole Abdul-Jabbar's No. 33 jersey. For the game that night, Abdul-Jabbar wore No. 50.

Although the 7-foot-2-inch (218-cm) Kareem wasn't at his best, he still finished with 27 points in the 31 minutes he played. The Lakers crushed the Bulls, 133–118.

In other words, the fans had no problem recognizing Kareem Abdul-Jabbar, even though he wasn't wearing his usual number. They just looked for the guy who was putting the ball in the basket more often than anyone else.

what's that number again?

What number was Babe Ruth wearing when he slammed his historic home run No. 60 on September 30, 1927?

Answer: He wasn't wearing any number! Baseball players didn't start wearing numbers on a regular basis until 1929.

Unforgettable

In 1962, the year the team was founded, the New York Mets had a catcher named Clarence "Choo-Choo" Coleman. Choo-Choo had trouble remembering names (and catching curve balls). Through his curious behavior, he became something of a legend.

When the Mets went to spring training in 1963, Charlie Neal was picked by the club to be Choo-Choo's roommate. Newspaper reporters went to Neal to get his reaction. "I'll bet he doesn't even remember me [from the season before]," said Neal, and he walked over to where Choo-Choo was seated.

"Do you know who I am?" Neal asked.

Choo-Choo looked Neal up and down. "Sure, I remember you," he said. "You're No. 4."

the one and only

"The Great One" is what Wayne Gretzky was called. When he announced his retirement on April 16, 1999, a veteran of twenty NHL seasons, Gretzky was hailed as the best player in hockey history. With his awesome skills as a playmaker, passer, and scorer, Gretzky had scored a record 1,072 goals, earned the league's Most Valuable Player award nine times, and played on four Stanley Cup championship teams.

Gretzky was also notable for his distinctive jersey number—No. 99. Gretzky started wearing No. 99 when he was a 16-year-old junior player for the Sault Ste. Marie Greyhounds, in Ontario.

When Gretzky joined the Greyhounds, he wanted No. 9, which had been worn by Gordie Howe, Gretzky's boyhood hero. No. 9 had also been worn by Bobby Hull of the Chicago Black Hawks and Maurice Richard of the Montreal Canadiens, two other Hall of Famers.

But No. 9 was not available. Someone then suggested that Wayne wear two 9s instead of one. Wayne agreed. At first, it was an oddity, but it wasn't very long before Gretzky had made No. 99 one of the best-known numbers in all of sports.

friendly gesture

In the seven seasons that he played for the Los Angeles Dodgers, catcher Mike Piazza had always worn No. 31. But after being dealt to the New York Mets in the spring of 1998, Piazza worried that his No. 31 was not going to be available. John Franco, the team's ace relief pitcher, had been wearing it for fifteen years.

Piazza had worried needlessly. When he arrived in the Mets clubhouse for the first time, a new Mets uniform was waiting for him, and No. 31 had been sewn on the back. Franco had voluntarily given up the number. "Hey, he's an All Star, a regular," Franco said. "I just wanted to make Mike feel welcome."

dis-honored

Tackle Ron Mix, 6 feet 4, 250 pounds (193 cm, 113 kg), was always a solid performer for the San Diego Chargers of the old American Football League. (The AFL operated from 1960 through 1969 and

then merged with the National Football League.) A rookie in 1960, Mix was named to *The Sporting News* All-Star team five times.

No one was surprised when, following his retirement in 1969, the Chargers announced that they were retiring Mix's uniform No. 74.

Mix did not play football in 1970. Then he decided he would like to give the game one more try. He signed with the Oakland Raiders in 1971. This move stunned his old team. Charger officials found it hard to believe that Mix would ever play for any other club but San Diego. They felt betrayed.

As a kind of punishment, the club decided to "un-retire" Mix's number. There was no pregame or halftime ceremony; they just did it. For the first time in sports history, a never-to-be-worn-again number got to be born again.

one of a kind

Robert Merrill, a noted performer for the Metropolitan Opera in New York City, was sometimes called upon to sing "The Star-Spangled Banner" before home games of the Yankees at Yankee Stadium. He often did it while wearing Yankee pinstripes. Merrill was issued a uniform number like no other: 1 1/2.

more 24s

Fans of the San Francisco Giants, formerly the New York Giants, identify No. 24 with the dazzling Willie Mays, who smacked 660 home runs during his career, which puts him third on the all-time list behind Hank Aaron and Babe Ruth. Besides being one of the leading sluggers in baseball history, Mays, a center fielder, was revered for his defensive skills.

There are two other No. 24s that should be cited. Both were worn by men who carved out important careers in government. One was Bill Bradley, who was elected U.S. senator from New Jersey in 1978 and reelected in 1984. Bradley wore No. 24 as a member of the New York Knicks from 1967 through 1977. An outstanding shooter, Bradley was a key contributor to the Knicks championship teams of 1970 and 1973.

Byron R. White, nicknamed "Whizzer," who served as an associate justice of the U.S. Supreme Court for more than a quarter of a century beginning in 1962, was another No. 24. White enjoyed a brief but notable career as a pro football running back. In 1938, when he played for the Pittsburgh Pirates (later to become the Steelers), White was the National Football League's leading rusher. White also wore No. 24 as a college player at the University of Colorado.

numbers expert

In 1998, after the Tennessee Lady Vols had won their third consecutive NCAA women's basketball championship, the team was invited to the White House to meet President Bill Clinton. The president singled out 6-foot-2, 167-pound (188-cm, 76-kg) Chamique Holdsclaw, the sport's Player of the Year in 1997, for special recognition. He compared "Meek," as she was known to her teammates, to Michael Jordan for playing a dominant role in every game of the season. "Incidentally," the president added, "she was wearing No. 23."

hall of fame

What are the most famous uniform numbers of all time? Each sports fan has his or her own list. But here's an attempt to identify the all-time greats without showing personal favoritism, or at least not too much of it.

- 1 — Pee Wee Reese, Brooklyn Dodgers; Ozzie Smith, St. Louis Cardinals
- 3 — Babe Ruth, New York Yankees
- 4 — Lou Gehrig, New York Yankees; Bobby Orr, Boston Bruins
- 5 — Joe DiMaggio, New York Yankees; Brooks Robinson, Baltimore Orioles; Johnny Bench, Cincinnati Reds
- 6 — Stan Musial, St. Louis Cardinals
- 7 — Mickey Mantle, New York Yankees
- 8 — Yogi Berra, New York Yankees
- 9 — Ted Williams, Boston Red Sox; Gordie Howe, Detroit Red Wings; Bobby Hull, Chicago Blackhawks
- 10 — Pelé, New York Cosmos
- 13 — Wilt Chamberlain, Philadelphia 76ers; Dan Marino, Miami Dolphins
- 14 — Ernie Banks, Chicago Cubs
- 16 — Joe Montana, San Francisco 49ers
- 19 — Johnny Unitas, Baltimore Colts; Bob Feller, Cleveland Indians
- 21 — Roberto Clemente, Pittsburgh Pirates; Sammy Sosa, Chicago Cubs; Warren Spahn, Milwaukee Braves
- 22 — Elgin Baylor, Los Angeles Lakers
- 23 — Michael Jordan, Chicago Bulls
- 24 — Willie Mays, San Francisco Giants
- 25 — Mark McGwire, St. Louis Cardinals
- 32 — Jim Brown, Cleveland Browns; O. J. Simpson, Buffalo Bills; Marcus Allen, Oakland Raiders; Sandy Koufax, Los Angeles Dodgers; Magic Johnson, Los Angeles Lakers
- 33 — Kareem Abdul-Jabbar, Milwaukee Bucks
- 34 — Walter Payton, Chicago Bears; Nolan Ryan, Houston Astros
- 42 — Jackie Robinson, Brooklyn Dodgers
- 44 — Hank Aaron, Atlanta Braves
- 77 — Red Grange, University of Illinois
- 99 — Wayne Gretzky, New York Rangers; George Mikan, Minneapolis Lakers

index